Contents

·········

CAF **HOW TO** GUIDE

THE

TREASURER'S HANDBOOK

A guide for small voluntary organisations

IAN CAULFEILD GRANT

**BASED ON THE SERIES
BY THE AUTHOR
PUBLISHED IN** *CHARITY*

©1996 Charities Aid Foundation

Published by Charities Aid Foundation
Kings Hill
West Malling
Kent ME19 4TA

Editor   Caroline Hartnell

Design and production   Eugenie Dodd Typographics

Printed and bound in Great Britain by Bell & Bain Limited, Glasgow

A catalogue record for this book is available from the British Library

ISBN 1–85934–018–0

CAF's web page:
http://www.charitynet.org

The publishers would like to thank John Rogers for his helpful
comments and suggestions.

About the author

·········

Ian Caulfeild Grant is a retired chartered accountant, who
has had dealings, in very practical ways, with all types and
sizes of fund. He was educated at Eastbourne College, Sussex,
and Auckland University. After qualifying as a chartered
accountant he chose to work in several types of environment in
order to broaden his experience. He is married and keeps busy
with writing and church interests.

Introduction

Part VI of the Charities Act 1993, which came into force on 1 March 1996, makes it a legal requirement for all registered charities to maintain accounting records and to retain them for at least six years. The Charities SORP (Statement of Recommended Practice) sets out recommendations on the way in which charities should prepare annual reports and accounts.

The treasurer of a charity is one of the trustees and is responsible, jointly with the other trustees, for controlling the management and administration of the charity. If trustees do not act prudently in managing the charity, they may be held personally liable for deficits incurred. It is therefore vital that the treasurer is able accurately to record and control the financial activity of the charity and advise the other trustees on the overall financial position.

The vast majority of the 180,000 charities registered with the Charity Commissioners for England and Wales are small. The person so often asked to be treasurer of a church, trust, club, association or other body is that helpful person who is willing to attend all the meetings and collect money from the other people who are also there. Very few people in this position, unless it is their profession (eg bankers or accountants), have accountancy experience. This handbook has been produced to assist such treasurers and others who are responsible for recording, controlling and reporting the financial activity of charities.

All registered charities are required to prepare annual accounts, but the format and content of the accounts vary according to the size of the charity (see pp 9–11 for details). This handbook is primarily aimed at treasurers of charities with total annual incomes of up to £100,000.

This book inevitably contains a number of accounting terms. These will usually be explained where they are used for the first time, but definitions are also given in the glossary at the end of the book.

CHAPTER ONE

Legal accounting requirements

The legal requirements relating to charity accounts are contained in Part VI of the Charities Act 1993 and the Charities (Accounts and Reports) Regulations 1995.

In addition to the legal requirements, the Charity Commission has produced a Statement of Recommended Practice (SORP), which sets out recommendations on the way in which charities should report annually on their activities. The SORP applies to all charities except where a more specialised SORP (such as the SORP for Registered Housing Associations) applies. The Charity Commissioners expect charities to comply with the SORP and their accounts to include an explanation of any divergence from the SORP. The Charity Commission has the power to institute an inquiry into the affairs of a charity that does not comply with the SORP and fails to provide a satisfactory explanation for not doing so.

The general accounting requirements vary according to the size of the charity in terms of its total income and/or total expenditure and are as follows.

All charities
- Must maintain accounting records and retain them for at least six years.
- Must prepare an annual report.
- Must prepare annual accounts and make them available to the public on request.

- Must be consistent in the treatment of like items within the year and from one year to the next.
- Must distinguish in their annual accounts between restricted, unrestricted and endowment funds (see Glossary for definitions of these terms).

Charities with income not over £1,000

- Are not required to register with the Charity Commission, but if they do so they will fall into the next category.

Charities with neither income nor expenditure over £10,000

- Annual accounts may be prepared on a Receipts and Payments basis.
- Accounts need not be independently examined or audited.
- The Charity Commission has power to require an audit in certain circumstances.

Charities with income not over £100,000 (but with either income or expenditure over £10,000)

- Annual accounts may be prepared on a Receipts and Payments basis.
- An annual return must be sent to the Charity Commission.
- Accounts must be subject to outside scrutiny but trustees may choose independent examination rather than audit.

Charities with neither income nor expenditure over £250,000 (but with income over £100,000)

- Annual accounts must be prepared on an accruals basis (Income and Expenditure Account).
- An annual return must be sent to the Charity Commission.
- Expenditure in the annual accounts must be analysed into:
  Direct charitable costs
  Fundraising and publicity
  Management and administration

- Accounts must be subject to outside scrutiny but trustees may choose independent examination rather than audit.

Charities with either income or expenditure over £250,000

- Annual accounts must be prepared on an accruals basis.
- An annual return must be sent to the Charity Commission.
- Expenditure in the annual accounts must be analysed into:
  Direct charitable costs
  Fundraising and publicity
  Management and administration
- Accounts must be audited by a registered auditor.

See page 68 for details of Charity Commission publications which give further details of the legal accounting requirements of charities.

CHAPTER TWO

Buying suitable books

There are a few simple rules which every aspiring treasurer should remember:

1 Buy suitable books for each type of transaction.

2 Bank all receipts intact (gross).

3 Have a cash float for all small payments. Never make payments out of receipts.

4 Reconcile cash records regularly.

5 Never pay money into your own bank account or make payments out of it.

6 Never sign blank cheques.

7 Always keep separate records for bankings.

8 Reconcile bank records regularly.

This chapter looks at the first of these.

Before doing anything else, you should make sure that you have suitable books for recording the financial affairs of the charity. How to use these books best will be discussed under subject headings.

The need to buy suitable books cannot be stressed enough. It should be remembered that the future financial viability of an organisation depends on the financial statements giving information in such a way that members are aware of the true state of affairs of the organisation. Forewarned is forearmed. If the charity is running out of money, something must be done about it *quickly*. If there is a surplus of money in the bank, it should be invested to earn income. The records should be in a form that enables the next treasurer to see exactly what has occurred. Buying the right books is the first step towards keeping clear records.

Where you wish to have a number of columns in which to analyse money received or spent, you should use a **columnar cash book** (also known as a **multi-column cash book**) or **computer spreadsheet**. You may like to have one book for each year. The books can then be taken away by the accountant and/or auditor during the preparation of the year-end accounts. Alternatively, you can use a looseleaf cash book so that the accountant/auditor takes away only the pages needed.

All sorts of columnar cash book are available. Some are quite thin (where there are not many entries), some thick; some have only four or five cash columns, others have 20 or more. When a book is referred to as, for example, a 'three-column cash book', this always refers to the number of cash columns.

The following are the books you are likely to need:

Cash receipts book and **cash payments book**   You may like to have separate books for these, or you may prefer to use one book, with receipts on one side and payments on the other. Separate receipts and payments books are recommended where a large number of items are recorded. Whichever option you choose, you will need a multi-column cash book with as many columns as you wish to analyse the receipts (see Example 1). The form in which you record how money is spent depends upon how many items there are. If there are many different types of expense and a large number of items, the accountant may wish an analysis of these payments to

Example 1 Multi-column cash book with five cash columns

be made. In that case, the use of a columnar cash book is again recommended.

Ring binder or other file for **Cash Control Account** forms.

Cash reconciliation book A small (A5) two-column cash book large enough to write down a short reconciliation periodically (see Example 2).

Bank receipts book and **bank payments book** As with recording cash receipts and payments, you may choose to use two separate books or you may prefer to use one. In either case, you will need a multi-column cash book(s), with as many columns as you wish to analyse the receipts and payments (see Example 1).

Bank reconciliation book A two-column cash book large enough (eg A5) to record the weekly bank reconciliation (see Example 2).

Bank Control Account book A ledger-style double-column book (if a full ledger is not already in use) (see Example 3).

Covenant reconciliation book A columnar cash book with at least six columns. If a computer spreadsheet program is used instead, the figures can easily be analysed into columns and these columns added automatically by the computer.

Example 2 A simple two-column cash book

Example 3 Ledger-style double-column book

CHAPTER THREE

Dealing with receipts

Recording receipts

All receipts, whether cash or cheques, must be recorded.

RULE 2 Bank all receipts intact (gross).

The recording of receipts should include:

The year, month and day (give the year sufficiently often to make it clear to what year the figures relate). If you use a separate cash book for each year, you will need to record only the month and day.

Details of the transaction Who the money was from and to what it refers.

Receipt number.

Amount.

You may wish to add further 'Description' columns (see Example 4). For example you may wish to have a column for:

- member's subscription number
- subscription period (eg 1994–95)
- covenantor's number
- expiry date of covenant

You may wish to add further 'Amount' columns. If you are a service-providing charity, for example, you may wish to have further columns for:

- fees from local authorities
- fees from private patients
- other contributions
- investment income

These columns may be further subdivided as much as you wish in order to give you more information about how the amounts are made up. 'Other contributions' could be divided into 'open days', 'coffee mornings', 'donations', 'covenants'. 'Investment income' should be divided between income received gross,

Example 4 Cash receipts book – service-providing charity

Date	Details	Receipt No	Total amount	Fees Local authorities	Private patients	Other contributions	Investment income
Sep 1	St Mary's House	2745	535.23	–	124.10	387.18	23.95
2	St Peter's House	3855	531.79	–	179.49	352.30	–
5	Abee City Council	3856	1,000.00	1,000.00	–	–	–

Example 5 Part of a page of a cash receipts book, showing further subdivisions of columns

	Other contributions					Investment income		
	Open days	Coffee mornings	Donations	Covenants	Other	Income gross	Company dividends	Govt stock
St Mary's House	98.23	56.21	88.00	90.00	54.74	–	23.95	–
St Peter's House	99.64	75.00	87.66	90.00	–	–	–	–

company dividends, etc, to allow easy analysis for the annual accounts (see Example 5).

If you are a grant-making charity, you may wish to have 'Amount' columns for donations, local councils, local organisations and investment income. These may also be subdivided as much as you wish. 'Donations' should definitely be divided between ordinary donations and those received under covenant.

If credit cards are accepted, these receipts should also be entered in a separate column.

Acknowledging receipts

An official receipt (and, preferably, a letter of thanks) should ideally be sent to all donors. The minimum amount for which a receipt is issued depends upon circumstances. No hard-and-fast rule should be set down: the smallest donations may involve large sacrifices on the part of those who make them.

An official receipt has several advantages. Everyone who gives money to a charity will want to know that their money has reached its intended destination. It places the charity in a poor light when a donor has to ask if their gift has been banked.

A receipt is proof that the right person has received the donation safely. If a letter is written (even a 'standard' letter, but quoting the person's name and the amount donated), it is also evidence to the staff and auditors of the charity that the person named on the receipt was the donor.

The receipt number should be recorded opposite the amount in the cash book. If receipts for more than one year are recorded in one book, the receipts should be numbered by year, for example 95/1, 95/2, 95/3, etc, and 96/1, 96/2, 96/3, etc.

CHAPTER FOUR

Handling a cash float

All cash payments should be made out of a **cash float** and recorded. The exact amount spent, supported by receipts or 'vouchers' (wherever possible), will then be reimbursed, bringing your float back to the original amount. This is known as the 'imprest' system.

RULE 3 Have a cash float for all small payments. Never make payments out of receipts.

How the 'float' or 'imprest' system works

1 You are given a 'float' of £50 out of which to make cash payments.

2 As each payment is made, you pay out money from the float, thus reducing the 'balance', which is the remaining 'cash-in-hand'. Every payment out of the £50 float thus reduces the cash-in-hand by that amount (eg a payment of £14.09 reduces the balance to £35.91.

3 You obtain a 'voucher' (the word 'receipt' can be confusing because it refers to money received) for each payment made. Hand these vouchers to the treasurer or cashier when you claim reimbursement of the amount spent.

4 You make further payments until you find, say, that you have only £2.68 cash-in-hand left: £47.32 has been spent out of the £50 float. You then complete an 'expenses claim

form' and obtain a reimbursement of the amount spent, which brings your float back to its original amount.

If there is a time-lag between claiming reimbursement and receiving the money, do not allow the cash-in-hand to run so low that you run out of money. It may be necessary to increase the amount of the float if you regularly run out of money after a short period of time.

Recording cash payments out of a cash float

You should keep a separate imprest cash book to record how the money is spent. The form in which this is done depends upon how many items there are. If there are many different types of expense, or a large number of items, you may wish to use a columnar cash book – a three-column cash book would probably be ideal – to analyse the payments (see Example 6).

The figures that are carried forward at the bottom of the page (£81.77, £81.77 and £50.00) are then brought forward to the top of the next page.

If you keep your imprest cash book in the form shown in Example 6, you can check the balance shown in the 'Balance (cash-in-hand)' column with the *actual* cash you hold (cash-in-hand) at any time. If there is any difference, you should *immediately* look for the error and correct it.

RULE 4 Reconcile cash records regularly.

This is called a 'cash reconciliation'. You should carry out cash reconciliations regularly – say once a week. For more on this, see page 22.

Example 6 Payments out of a cash float recorded in a three-column cash book

Date	Details	Voucher number	Pay-ments £	Reimburse-ments £	Balance (cash-in-hand) £
1994					
1 Sep	*Balance brought forward*				50.00
1 Sep	Photocopying	(P1)	14.09	–	35.91
2 Sep	Printing leaflet	(P2)	10.00	–	25.91
2 Sep	Envelopes	(P3)	2.75	–	23.16
3 Sep	Stamps	(P4)	0.84	–	22.32
4 Sep	Advert in newspaper	(P5)	3.32	–	19.00
5 Sep	Cleaning materials	(P6)	9.93	–	9.07
6 Sep	Cash books	(P7)	6.39	–	2.68
6 Sep	Reimbursement	(R1)	–	47.32	50.00
8 Sep	Petrol (travelling to branch at Exeter)	(P8)	12.45	–	37.55
10 Sep	Advertising copy	(P9)	11.26	–	26.29
12 Sep	Photocopying	(P10)	2.75	–	23.54
13 Sep	A4 paper	(P11)	3.42	–	20.12
15 Sep	Ballpoint pens	(P12)	0.32	–	19.80
15 Sep	Stamps	(P13)	4.25	–	15.55
19 Sep	Reimbursement	(R2)	–	34.45	50.00
	Carried forward		81.77	81.77	50.00

Note P = payment. R = receipt.

Cash Control Accounts

A 'Cash Control Account' shows:

1 Cash-in-hand at the beginning of the period (opening balance) *plus*

2 cash received in the period (receipts) *less*

3 cash banked or spent during the period (payments) *equals*

4 cash-in-hand at the end of the period (closing balance).

The closing balance must reconcile (agree) with the actual cash-in-hand at the time when you prepare the account.

Example 7 Cash Control Account where 'Payments' are all bankings

	Debit	£	Credit	£
31.8.95	Opening balance	123.45	Payments – bankings	423.98
	Receipts	345.76	Closing balance	45.23
	Total	**469.21**	**Total**	**469.21**
7.9.95	Opening balance b/f	45.23		

Example 8 Cash Control Account where 'Payments' include bankings and the issue of cash floats

	Debit	£	£	Credit	£	£
31.8.95	Opening balance		123.45			
	Receipts – donations			Payments – bankings		
	Dept A	3,564.00		Dept A	3,564.00	
	Dept B	1,000.00		Dept B	1,000.00	
	Dept C	5,874.50	10,438.50	Dept C	5,874.50	10,438.50
			10,561.95			
	Receipts – floats returned			Payments – floats granted		
				Dept A	1,000.00	
	Dept B		2,000.00	Dept B	230.00	
				Dept C	533.00	1,763.00
						12,201.50
				Closing balance		360.45
	Total		**12,561.95**			**12,561.95**
7.9.95	Opening balance b/f		360.45			

Example 7 shows how an organisation would complete a Cash Control Account where 'Payments' are all bankings because a separate float is kept for cash payments. Example 8 shows a Cash Control Account where 'Payments' include the issue of cash floats as well as bankings. If cash payments have to be made, a cash payments book should be kept and the daily total from that recorded in the Cash Control Account.

Unless you record this information in a formal ledger, I suggest that you decide on a form that suits your requirements and have a supply of forms printed or photocopied so that you have them available at the end of each period. They should be filed in a ledger, lever arch file or ring binder.

Cash reconciliations

As already explained, a cash reconciliation consists simply of checking that your cash-in-hand agrees (reconciles) exactly with the closing balance in your imprest cash book, Cash Control Account or other written record.

If you find that the closing balance often does not agree exactly with your cash-in-hand, a book should be kept in which cash reconciliations are recorded in a manner similar to that which will be explained for bank reconciliations (see pp 26–34).

The reason for a discrepancy may simply be an adding mistake or a payment not recorded.

CHAPTER FIVE

Recording bank transactions

Banking receipts

All money received – cash (notes and coins) or cheques – should be deposited in a bank account in the name of the charity.

RULE 5 Never pay money into your own bank account or make payments out of it.

All receipts should be banked as soon as received. If cheques are not banked for weeks or even months after being sent to a charity, this suggests to the donor that the charity did not really need their money.

Making payments

Cheques should never be signed by a person authorised to sign cheques *before* the name of the person to whom the cheque is payable (the payee) and the amount have been written on the cheque.

RULE 6 Never sign blank cheques.

The main purpose of having two or more signatories (people authorised to sign cheques) is to ensure that proper control is maintained over (1) to whom the money is being paid and (2) how much is being paid. Following correct procedures ensures that the payment is made to the person named on the cheque and for the amount shown.

The cheque signatory must be satisfied that the payment is due and is for the correct amount. The word 'PAID' should be hand-written (not rubber-stamped) on the invoice by the signatory and preferably initialled so that that person can later be satisfied that it was they who checked these two points and signed the cheque accordingly.

Cheque frauds almost invariably occur because someone has not ensured proper control of the signing of cheques. If one signatory goes on holiday for a fortnight, it should be no great problem to arrange for someone else to be temporary signatory.

Recording transactions

When recording bank receipts and payments, one important consideration is ease of reconciliation with the bank statements.

RULE 7 Always keep separate records for bankings.

Example 9 Bank account cash book that follows the layout of a bank statement

Date	Details	Chq no	Payments £	Receipts £	Balance £
1995					
1 Sep	Balance brought forward				934.75
1 Sep	Cash banked		–	✓100.00	1,034.75
1 Sep		100147	✓229.43	–	805.32
1 Sep		100148	✓201.73	–	603.59
1 Sep		100149	✓5.98	–	597.61
3 Sep	Cash banked		–	✓234.56	832.17
4 Sep		100150	142.98	–	689.19
4 Sep		100151	10.87	–	678.32
5 Sep	PRQ Trust grant		–	✓1,000.00	1,678.32
5 Sep	BT STO		✓36.00	–	1,642.32
6 Sep	Cash banked		–	213.76	1,856.08

If there are not many receipts or payments, it is adequate to record both receipts and payments in a cash book which basically follows the layout of the bank statement (see Example 9; the ticks beside some of the items in Examples 9 and 10 will be explained on pp 28–31 under the heading of 'Bank reconciliations'). You may, however, find it easier to record receipts and payments on opposite pages of your cash book, or even in two separate books. If you record receipts and payments separately (whether on different pages or in different books), you will also need to have, as one of your ledger accounts, a **Bank Control Account**.

Example 10 shows what a bank statement covering the same period might look like where the amounts are not great.

Example 10 Bank statement of a small charity

XYZ Project Current Account

Statement of account 98765432

PRQ Bank plc
High Street

Diary 1Sep95

MR A B C
1 Station Road
X Town XT12 3AA

No 108

Date	Details	Withdrawals	Deposits	Balance
1995				
1 Sep	Balance forward			1,202.80
1 Sep	100143	157.87		1,044.93
3 Sep	100146	99.23		
3 Sep	100145	10.95		
3 Sep	Xtown, High Street		✓100.00	1,034.75
4 Sep	100147	✓229.43		
4 Sep	100149	✓5.98		
4 Sep	100148	✓201.73		
4 Sep	XTown, High Street		✓234.56	832.17
5 Sep	Midland 407027		✓1,000.00	
5 Sep	BT STO	✓36.00		1,796.17

Do not allow your bank to tell you how often you will receive a
bank statement. Tell them how often you want them, generally
weekly or monthly. In very rare circumstances (eg with a
deposit account with only a few transactions a year), you might
agree to have a statement only when a transaction occurs.

Bank Control Accounts

If you keep separate receipts and payments records, then it will
be necessary to have a 'Bank Control Account' or similar record
in order to know what the overall position is.

A Bank Control Account takes exactly the same form as a Cash
Control Account, described on pages 20–22: opening balance
plus receipts *less* payments *equals* closing balance (see Example
11).

Example 11 Bank Control Account

Account Number 98765432

	Debit	£	Credit	£
31.8.95	Opening balance	934.75	Payments (daily)	626.99
	Receipts (daily)	1,548.32	Closing balance	1,856.08
	Total	**2,483.07**	**Total**	**2,483.07**
7.9.95	Opening balance b/f	1,856.08		

Bank reconciliations

Why you should do regular reconciliations

Now turn to the example of a simple bank statement (Example
10). The danger of looking at the last entry in the right-hand
column (£1,796.17) is that it is all too easy to think that this is
the actual money you have in the bank. It is very seldom that it
reflects the true position. The closing amount on the bank
statement must be regularly reconciled with the bank account

cash book balance (or Bank Control Account) to ensure that your bank account cash book balance (or Bank Control Account) shows the charity's true financial position.

RULE 8 Reconcile bank records regularly.

A 'bank reconciliation' is a simple way to check the bank's records against yours. The records do not really disagree: it is just that they do not include exactly the same transactions for the same periods of time. If you had no further transactions for a couple of weeks, the bank's records and yours would then agree.

The two main aims of bank reconciliations are:

- to check that your bank account cash book (or Bank Control Account) balance is correct;
- to ascertain your latest credit balance (or overdraft) at the bank.

Bank reconciliations are a vital part of all accounting practice. Regular reconciliations should be carried out.

Some tips for doing successful bank reconciliations

It is easy to reconcile your bank balance with your bank account cash book if you stick to a few simple rules:

- Always keep the main bank account cash book entirely for bank transactions. Every item in the bank account cash book should then appear, at some time or other, on the bank statement, and vice versa.
- Follow the same procedure every time you do a bank reconciliation. The form (pattern or design) in which the bank reconciliation is written should always be the same.
- Keep a note book for reconciliations – a simple two-column cash book is ideal (Example 2). You then have a permanent record and can refer back to it. A labour-saving method is to have a ring binder and use a standard form (photocopied from an original) which you complete each time you do the reconciliation.

Note There are two types of reconciliation, depending on whether your bank statement shows a credit balance or an overdraft. What follows is an account of how to do a bank reconciliation when your bank statement shows a credit balance. For reconciliations when your statement shows an overdraft, see pages 32–33.

What you will need

When you carry out your bank reconciliation you will need to have four sets of documents side by side:

- bank receipts book
- bank reconciliation book
- bank statement
- bank payments book

Before starting the reconciliation, ensure that the bank account cash book is fully up to date. Enter all cheques drawn; all bankings; all transfers requested from other accounts (eg from deposit to current); any other adjustments you have asked the bank to make which you have not yet recorded in the cash book.

Rule a line across the bank statement underneath the last entry in the period for which you are doing the reconciliation. Usually this will be underneath the last entry on the statement (because you will be doing the reconciliation at the time you receive the latest bank statement).

The procedure to follow

You will be comparing the amounts on the bank statement either with those in your bank account cash book (or other record of bank transactions) or with those in the previous bank reconciliation. These two sets of records should be ticked against each other. For the sake of clarity:

- Use a different coloured pen each time you carry out a reconciliation. In the first week (or shorter/longer period), use a red pen; in the second, a green pen; in the third, an orange pen. In the fourth, revert to red, then to green, and so on.

- Put your tick as near the figure as possible. The bank statement will not have grid lines (column rules) but your bank account cash book may. If so, it is tidier to put your ticks neatly down the grid line. The examples show ticks on the left-hand side of the figures, but you may find it easier to tick on the right-hand side.

Always work **from** the bank statement **to** the cash book or to the previous bank reconciliation. Start with the last figure on the bank statement (or the last figure in the period for which you are doing the reconciliation).

Receipts

First, deal with all the amounts under the heading of 'Deposits' or 'Receipts' on the bank statement, ticking each amount, in turn, from the bank statement to the cash book or to the previous bank reconciliation. Receipts that you did not tick off in your cash book when you did the previous reconciliation because they had not yet been credited by the bank will be shown on the previous reconciliation as 'deposits not yet credited'. These will now be ticked off against the bank statement (or carried forward on the reconciliation you are now doing).

You may need to enter items in your cash book which were on the bank statement but not in your cash book (eg fees, subscriptions and other amounts paid direct into your account, or interest paid on interest-bearing bank accounts). If so, tick off these items also.

Then start a new bank reconciliation, heading it with the date of the reconciliation (eg week ended 7 June 1995). Fill in the amount of the credit balance (see pp 32–33 if there is an overdraft) per the bank statement followed by any receipts (deposits) which you have not ticked off in your bank receipts cash book received at any time *before* the date of the reconciliation. These receipts have not, of course, been credited by the bank (which is why you have not ticked them).

Payments

Next deal with all the amounts under the heading of 'Payments' or 'Withdrawals' on the bank statement, ticking each amount, in turn, from the bank statement to the cash book or to the previous bank reconciliation. Payments that you did not tick off in your cash book when you did the previous reconciliation because the cheques had not yet been presented at the bank will be shown on the previous reconciliation as 'outstanding payments'. These will now be ticked off against the bank statement or carried forward on the reconciliation you are now doing. (If someone to whom you have paid a cheque omits to pay

Example 12 Bank reconciliation at the start of the period

Bank reconciliation as at 31 August 1995

		£	£
1	Balance per bank statement		1,202.80
2	Add deposits not yet credited		
3	Subtotal		1,202.80
4	Deduct outstanding payments		
	cheque number 100143	157.87	
	cheque number 100145	10.95	
	cheque number 100146	99.23	268.05
5	Balance per cash book (or Bank Control Account)		934.75

Example 13 Bank reconciliation at the end of the period

Bank reconciliation as at 7 September 1995

		£	£
1	Balance per bank statement		1,796.17
2	Add deposits not yet credited		
	6 September 1995		213.76
3	Subtotal		2,009.93
4	Deduct outstanding payments		
	cheque number 100150	142.98	
	cheque number 100151	10.87	153.85
5	Balance per cash book (or Bank Control Account)		1,856.08

it in for some time, the payment will be carried forward as an outstanding payment until it is finally presented.)

You may need to enter items in your cash book which were on the bank statement but not in your cash book (eg bank charges made by the bank of which you were not aware – for using a safe deposit box, having an overdraft, stopping cheques, electronic transfer of funds – or direct debits: although you will have been advised of the amount, you may not have entered it in your cash book). If so, tick off these items also.

Record on the bank reconciliation all payments which you have not ticked off in your bank payments cash book (because the cheques have not yet been presented at the bank).

Examples 12 and 13 show two bank reconciliations, one carried out at the start of the period covered by the bank account cash book and bank statement shown in Examples 9 and 10 and the other at the end.

Checking the results

Finally, see that the result on your bank reconciliation agrees with the closing balance in your bank account cash book or Bank Control Account. If there is any difference, go back and check that you have not omitted any item or added the columns incorrectly.

If you still do not reconcile, and you have checked all cross-references (bank statement to cash book), go back to the beginning and check to see that you have carried out all the proper procedures, including noting whether or not a 'balance' has become an 'overdraft' or vice versa.

When the receipts consist largely of fees or subscriptions credited direct to the charity's bank account, each of which is for an identical amount, it is obviously vital to be extremely careful to mark off the correct two amounts (in the bank statement and the cash book).

Your system should be such that you know exactly who gave a fee or subscription and mark off that specific item in the bank statement. Never simply mark off one similar amount to another in the order in which they appear, otherwise you will not know whose subscription has not been credited to the bank account.

Reconciliations where the bank statement shows an overdraft

Where you have an overdraft (debit balance) on the bank statement, the format for the reconciliation will differ from that for a credit balance, as shown in Example 14.

Example 14 Bank reconciliation where the bank statement shows an overdraft

Bank reconciliation as at 31 August 1995

	£	£
1 Overdraft per bank statement		9,458.25
4 Add outstanding payments		
cheque number 100194	200.00	
cheque number 100195	123.45	
cheque number 100196	96.52	419.97
3 Subtotal		9,878.22
2 Deduct deposits not yet credited		1,452.94
5 Overdraft per cash book (or Bank Control Account)		8,425.28

Where the bank statement shows an overdraft, the Bank Control Account will also take a different form (see Example 15).

The key difference lies in the order in which the reconciliation deals with outstanding payments and deposits not yet credited.

If your bank statement shows a *credit* balance, all cheques drawn by you (and other outgoings) not yet deducted by the bank are going to *reduce* the balance; if there is an *overdraft* (a debit balance), outgoings are going to *increase* the overdraft. Everything stems from this concept.

Example 15 Bank Control Account where the bank statement shows an overdraft

Account Number 98765432

	Debit	£	Credit	£
31.8.95	Opening balance	934.75	Payments (daily)	12,908.35
	Receipts (daily)	3,548.32		
6.9.95	Closing overdraft	8,425.28		
	Total	**12,908.35**	**Total**	**12,908.35**
7.9.95			Opening overdraft b/f	8,425.28

It is vital always to start the bank reconciliation with the last figure shown on the latest bank statement. With the credit bank reconciliation, the deposits not yet credited are dealt with first, as these *add* to the balance. The *opposite* applies in this overdraft reconciliation: outstanding payments add to the overdraft and so are dealt with first.

Once again, if you find that the 'balance per cash book' in your bank reconciliation does not agree with your *actual* final balance in the bank account cash book or Bank Control Account, the explanation must be that some item(s) has/have been missed or there is an error in addition.

Where a balance has become an overdraft or vice versa

If the closing balance on the bank statement is reduced by outstanding cheques to such an extent that you end up with a debit (overdraft) figure, obviously your cash book or Bank Control Account will show an overdraft. In this situation (where the bank statement is in credit but the cash book shows an overdraft), use the format for the reconciliation where there is a credit balance on the bank statement (Examples 12 and 13).

On the other hand, you may find that the overdraft on the bank statement is reduced by outstanding deposits (receipts) to such an extent that you end up with a credit balance in your cash book or Bank Control Account. In that case, use the format for the reconciliation where there is an overdraft shown on the bank statement (Example 14).

CHAPTER SIX

Budgeting and cash flow forecasting

Budgeting

Before the start of each year a budget should be prepared to show how much it is estimated that the charity needs to spend in order to carry out its activities in the coming year. If the level of the income is known, this should be included in the budget, but often the expenditure budget will be used for fundraising purposes, for example to support applications for grants.

The budget should be prepared by reviewing expenditure in the current year and estimating how it is likely to change in the coming year in terms of different levels of activity, estimated inflation and known increases such as for salaries where the scales are known.

During the year, say once a quarter, the actual income and expenditure should be compared to the budgeted income and expenditure. Any significant variations should be investigated to enable remedial action to be taken by the trustees if necessary. Quarterly – or perhaps monthly – budgets need to be prepared to enable such comparisons to be made.

Cash flow forecasting

A budget shows income and expenditure which is expected to be earned and incurred in the year. However, the timing of the actual receipts and payments will be different from that shown in the budget. It is therefore advisable for a cash flow forecast to be prepared.

Whereas the budget will spread some items of income and expenditure evenly over the year (for example an insurance premium of £600 per year might be shown as £50 per month), the cash flow forecast will show the whole £600 in the expected month of payment. Similarly, a grant of £12,000 receivable in the first month of the year will be shown in that month in the cash flow forecast but would be shown as £1,000 per month in the budget.

The preparation and regular monitoring of cash flow forecasts will enable the trustees to plan any short-term bank borrowings that may be required and to invest any surplus funds for periods indicated by the forecast.

Working out your present financial position

You use the same basic framework for a cash flow forecast as you would for working out your present financial position.

Example 16 Simple statement of your financial position at the end of a week

	£
I started the week with	10.23
I received	98.67
	108.90
I spent	52.56
I ended the week with	56.34

Example 16 shows how much money you had at the beginning and end of the week, and how much you received and spent during the week. Example 17 shows another way you could make the statement.

Example 17 Alternative statement of your financial position at the end of a week

	£	£
1 I received	98.67	
2 I spent	52.56	
3 Net receipts (excess of receipts over payments)		46.11
4 I started the week with		10.23
5 I ended the week with		56.34

This basic framework, shown in Example 18, is also the framework you will use when you come to doing cash flow forecasts (see below) and Receipts and Payments Accounts (see Chapter 7).

Example 18 Basic framework for statement of present financial position or cash flow forecast

1 Receipts	1	
2 Payments	2	
3 Net receipts (1 minus 2)		3
4 Opening balance		4
5 Closing balance		5

Preparing a cash flow forecast

You can work out how much money you should have at certain dates in the future using the basic framework shown in Example 18. If you have a number of items that fall under one of the headings, then you simply list them under one another.

The cash flow forecast shown in Example 19 gives monthly budgets or forecasts.

Example 19 Cash flow forecasts for six months

	Sep 1995	Oct 1995	Nov 1995	Dec 1995	Jan 1996	Feb 1996	Total
Receipts	£	£	£	£	£	£	£
Central Finance Board	1,000.00	–	–	–	–	–	1,000.00
Grants and donations	133.34	2,385.38	250.00	383.34	3,750.00	250.00	7,152.06
Rent	195.20	195.20	195.20	201.87	201.87	201.87	1,191.21
Total receipts (1)	1,328.54	2,580.58	445.20	585.21	3,951.87	451.87	9,343.27
Payments							
Advertising	–	70.00	–	–	–	40.00	110.00
Capital payments	–	–	–	–	–	–	–
Heat, light and power	93.50	93.50	93.50	93.50	93.50	93.50	561.00
House expenses	143.35	232.99	140.48	143.35	143.35	143.35	946.87
Insurance	–	–	–	130.00	–	–	130.00
Interest charges	–	–	–	–	–	–	–
Payments to creditors	–	–	–	–	–	–	–
Postage	20.00	20.00	20.00	20.00	20.00	20.00	120.00

Printing and stationery	201.73	–	–	–	–	–	201.73
Professional fees	–	–	–	–	–	–	–
Rent, rates and water	146.87	129.49	60.00	60.00	60.00	60.00	516.36
Repairs and renewals	–	–	–	–	–	–	–
Salaries and wages	813.30	1,118.68	1,119.18	997.87	997.87	997.87	6,044.76
Telephone	32.00	32.00	32.00	32.00	32.00	32.00	192.00
Transport	12.13	230.62	168.00	38.00	268.00	168.00	884.75
Total payments (2)	1,462.88	1,927.27	1,633.16	1,514.72	1,614.72	1,554.72	9,707.47
Net cash flow (1–2)	(134.34)	653.31	(1,187.96)	(929.51)	2,337.15	(1,102.85)	(364.20)
Opening bank balance/(overdraft)	471.96	337.62	990.93	(197.03)	(1,126.54)	1,210.61	471.96
Closing bank balance/(overdraft)	337.62	990.93	(197.03)	(1,126.54)	1,210.61	107.76	107.76

CHAPTER SEVEN

Receipts and Payments Accounts

Receipts and Payments Accounts show us the cash position of the charity but they do not show the overall financial position. They are similar in format to the cash flow forecasts discussed in Chapter 6.

The sets of items **1**, **2** and **3** in Example 20 comprise the Receipts and Payments Account; items **4** and **5** comprise the Balance Sheet, which is explained on pages 45–46.

The Receipts and Payments Account provides us with the 'excess of receipts over payments' (or 'excess of payments over receipts').

The 'details' (eg 'fees', 'rent') are listed in alphabetical order. This makes it much easier to find an item quickly when you want to consider it at a meeting.

As mentioned on page 10, all charities are legally required to distinguish in their accounts between **unrestricted**, **restricted** and **endowment** funds. For the sake of simplicity, the examples in this chapter assume that all funds received are unrestricted, which means that they can be spent at the discretion of the trustees for the purposes of the charity.

If your charity also receives restricted funds (funds that can be spent only for a specific purpose, stated by the donor), you will need to show these in a separate column. Small charities are unlikely to have any endowment funds (see Glossary for definition).

Example 20 Receipts and Payments Account

Year to 31.8.94 £	£		£	Year to 31.8.95 £
		1 *Receipts*		
	98.45	Annual 'Open Day'	123.45	
	79.43	Fees	86.67	
	15.65	Investment income	12.65	
217.09	23.56	Sales in the shop	24.87	247.64
		2 *Payments*		
	19.87	'Open Day' costs	25.87	
	24.93	Purchases for shop	21.45	
	50.00	Rent of office	50.00	
94.80				97.32
122.29		**3** *Net receipts* (excess of receipts over payments)		150.32

Balance Sheet as at 31 August 1995

31.8.94			*31.8.95*
	Assets		
78.25	Cash-in-hand		82.32
718.37	Money at bank		934.75
796.62			1,017.07
4,421.13	Furniture		4,351.00
5,217.75			5,368.07
	Liabilities		
	Accumulated Fund: XYZ Fund		
5,095.46	**4** Opening balance		5,217.75
122.29	**3** Excess of receipts over payments		150.32
5,217.75	**5** Closing balance		5,368.07

Example 21 Receipts and Payments Account

Year to 31.8.94 £	£		£	Year to 31.8.95 £
		1 Receipts		
	98.45	Annual 'Open Day'	123.45	
	79.43	Fees	86.67	
	15.65	Investment income	12.65	
217.09	23.56	Sales in the shop	24.87	247.64
		2 Payments		
	100.00	Capitation	160.00	
	19.87	'Open Day' costs	25.87	
	24.93	Purchases for shop	21.45	
	50.00	Rent of office	50.00	
194.80				257.32
22.29		**3** Net receipts (excess of receipts over payments)		(9,68)

Balance Sheet as at 31 August 1995

31.8.94			31.8.95
	Assets		
78.25	Cash-in-hand		82.32
618.37	Money at bank		674.75
696.62			757.07
4,421.13	Furniture		4,351.00
5,117.75			5,108.07
	Liabilities		
	Accumulated Fund: XYZ Fund		
5,095.46	**4** Opening balance		5,117.75
22.29	**3** Excess of receipts over payments		(9.68)
5,117.75	**5** Closing balance		5,108.07

Accounts should always follow the same accounting principles year after year. If any change is made, it *must* be explained in notes attached to the accounts. This is known as the 'consistency concept'. It dictates that similar items, within each accounting period and from one period to the next, are treated consistently (in a similar accounting manner).

In practice, there may well be periods when total payments exceed total receipts. This will result in negative net receipts (excess of payments over receipts) and, therefore, in net payments. It is best to keep to the framework and show the net payments in brackets. (Brackets are used by accountants to indicate a negative figure.)

Let us say, using the same figures as in Example 20, that there is a capitation fee payable to your central body (if your group is part of a national organisation) made up of a fixed amount per member. The results are shown in Example 21.

Comparing one year with another
....
One of the most important uses of a set of accounts is to see how the amounts for specific items change from one year to another. You will see from Example 22 that the trend is consistent for several years and then changes drastically. Your trustees or members should take note of these changes. Everyone should query why fees fall from £18,000 in 1993 to £7,000 in 1994 and then rise to £35,000 in 1995. In fact, some fees for 1994 were not received until 1995 – this had not happened in previous years. If you look at the figures for 1994 and 1995, you will see that the total for the two years is £42,000: £13,000 of the 1994 fees were received in 1994. Fluctuations in investment income would also need explaining.

People looking at the accounts should also note that the support costs went up from £1,900 in 1992 to £2,500 in 1993 and fell again to £1,800 in 1994. In this case members should be told that the £2,500 in 1993 includes £600 worth of stock carried forward to 1994, and that 1994 includes £600 carried forward to 1995, and that 1995 includes £500 that will be carried forward to 1996.

Example 22 Receipts and Payments Accounts for five years

	1991 £	1992 £	1993 £	1994 £	1995 £
1 *Receipts*					
Fees	11,100	15,000	18,000	7,000	35,000
Other contributions	1,200	1,000	1,500	1,700	1,900
Investment income	2,100	2,200	3,000	600	3,400
	14,400	18,200	22,500	9,300	40,300
2 *Payments*					
Community services	1,000	1,300	1,400	1,500	1,600
Purchase of equipment	–	13,600	–	–	29,000
Residential care	3,000	3,000	4,000	4,000	5,000
Support services	1,800	1,900	2,500	1,800	1,900
	5,800	19,800	7,900	7,300	37,500
3 *Excess of receipts over payments*	8,600	(1,600)	14,600	2,000	2,800
4 *Excess of receipts over payments excluding the purchase of equipment*	8,600	12,000	14,600	2,000	31,800

Note that a Receipts and Payments Account does *not* include any provisions for outstanding debtors (money due **to** the charity) or creditors (amounts owing **by** the charity), nor does it take account of stock or depreciation (see pp 48–49). That is why it is called a Receipts and Payments Account: it deals *only* with receipts and payments within the period covered by the accounts.

When we look at Income and Expenditure Accounts in Chapter 8, we will see that these include provisions for debtors, creditors, stock and depreciation. The figures are then shown in the years to which they actually relate, and the fluctuations evident in the Receipts and Payments Account disappear.

This also applies to accounts which may be called 'Profit and Loss Accounts' (used by organisations that buy goods and services), 'Statements of Financial Activities', etc.

Whatever type of account is used, it is very important that the reader of those accounts knows whether they include 'provisions' or not.

The Balance Sheet

You can balance accounts in many ways and at many stages, but for the present discussion it is enough to describe the year-end accounts.

Let us start with a very simple example, likening the Balance Sheet to the two sides of a set of scales. Think of yourself on a shopping trip. You leave home with £17.75 (opening balance), get £247.64 out of your building society (receipts) and spend £257.32 (payments), which means that you spend a net amount of £9.68. You come home with £8.07 (closing balance). Example 23 shows how these figures might be presented as a Balance Sheet. In this case the Balance Sheet is simply showing that the cash-in-hand you actually have at the end of the shopping trip (your assets) corresponds with the closing balance on the liabilities side. You therefore know that your accounts are balanced.

You will notice that in Example 23, the liabilities (credits) are on the left-hand side and the assets (debits) on the right. All other examples of Balance Sheets in this handbook show the liabilities

Example 23 Balance Sheet drawn up following a shopping trip

Liabilities		Assets
Accumulated Fund		Cash-in-hand
£		£
17.75	Opening balance	17.75
9.68	Less excess of payments over receipts	9.68
8.07	Closing balance	8.07

under the assets, as this is the way accounts are usually presented. Example 23 shows liabilities and assets side by side – a more old-fashioned form of presentation – because it makes the balancing of the two sides clearer.

A charity's accounts are based on exactly the same principle. Instead of you, there is the body of trustees (or other body of people) who have paid in or are responsible for a sum of money which is recorded under the heading of 'Accumulated Fund'. That is on the liabilities side of the Balance Sheet: the charity has the *liability* to pay out that money in the event of it ceasing to operate or you ceasing to be responsible for any money which you hold. The cash-in-hand, money at the bank and equipment shown in Examples 20 and 21 are the charity's assets which are exactly equal to its liabilities (hence the name 'Balance Sheet').

If your Balance Sheet does not balance, you know that you have made mistakes. In order to find where the error is, subtract the lower total from the higher side of the Balance Sheet. See if this amount is a figure which you have omitted to record in the Receipts and Payments Account or the Balance Sheet.

Going back to Example 21, if the difference is £160, then you might suspect that you have omitted the 'Capitation' from the Receipts and Payments Account. If the left-hand side is £19.36 higher than the right, you might suspect that you have added the £9.68 (half of £19.36) instead of deducting it from the opening balance on the Accumulated Fund.

If that fails, *check all the figures*. Ultimately both sides must balance. If you still do not balance, go back to the basic principles and ensure that you understand what you are doing wrong.

CHAPTER EIGHT
....

Income and Expenditure Accounts

Income and Expenditure Accounts provide a better picture of the affairs of an organisation than Receipts and Payments Accounts because they present a more complete picture.

- A Receipts and Payments Account deals with money-only transactions during the financial period covered.

- An Income and Expenditure Account contains this information but is then adjusted to include opening and closing debtors, creditors, stock and depreciation in order to provide a true picture of the exact amounts which apply to that period (which relate *directly* to that period).

- The Balance Sheet, when you prepare an Income and Expenditure Account, also includes stock, debtors, creditors and depreciation, these being the adjustments made to your Receipts and Payments Account to convert it to an Income and Expenditure Account.

As mentioned on page 10, all charities are legally required to distinguish in their accounts between **unrestricted**, **restricted** and **endowment** funds. For the sake of simplicity, the examples in this chapter assume that all funds received are unrestricted, which means that they can be spent at the discretion of the trustees for the purposes of the charity.

If your charity also receives restricted funds (funds that can be spent only for a specific purpose, stated by the donor), you will need to show these in a separate column. Small charities are unlikely to have any endowment funds (see Glossary for definition).

Before turning to the preparation of the Income and Expenditure Account, we should look at how equipment is dealt with in accounts.

Equipment as an asset

Returning to the Receipts and Payments Account shown in Example 22, you will see that equipment was bought in 1992 and 1995. Consideration should be given to the life expectancy of this equipment. If it will not last more than two or three years, it is reasonable to include its cost in the revenue accounts in the year in which it was bought. If the cost is relatively large compared with other payments and the purchases are spasmodic, as they are here, the cost of the equipment should be shown in the Balance Sheet as an asset.

In this case the cost is divided equally over the estimated life of the equipment and the annual amount is charged as 'depreciation' in the Income and Expenditure Account. In the year in which it is sold or scrapped an adjustment will be made to take account of any money received when that occurs.

The equipment bought in the year ended 1995, for example, cost £29,000 and had an estimated life of ten years. This cost will therefore be written off as depreciation equally over ten years at the rate of £2,900 per annum in the Income and Expenditure Account. A similar amount is deducted from the value of the equipment as shown in the Balance Sheet.

Any amount received when it is disposed of after its estimated life of ten years will be shown as a receipt in the Income and Expenditure Account; the amount received will increase cash-in-hand on the Balance Sheet by the same amount.

As it turns out, the equipment is well looked after and is not scrapped until the year ended 2007, when the scrap is sold for £200 (see Example 24).

Example 24 Depreciation of equipment over ten years

Year		Balance Sheet value at start of year £	Depreciation charged to Income and Expenditure Account £		Balance Sheet value at end of year £
1995	Cost	29,000	(2,900)		26,100
1996		26,100	(2,900)		23,200
1997		23,200	(2,900)		20,300
1998		20,300	(2,900)		17,400
1999		17,400	(2,900)		14,500
2000		14,500	(2,900)		11,600
2001		11,600	(2,900)		8,700
2002		8,700	(2,900)		5,800
2003		5,800	(2,900)		2,900
2004		2,900	(2,900)		–
2005		–	–		–
2006		–	–		–
2007		–	200	Cash	200

The Income and Expenditure Account
·········
We will now incorporate the various adjustments that had to be made to the Receipts and Payments Account to convert it to an Income and Expenditure Account. Example 25 shows a Receipts and Payments Account for the year ended 31 August 1995, while Example 26 shows the Income and Expenditure account for the same year. The key differences between the two are as follows:

- The figures for fees have been adjusted in Example 26 to show the fees under the years to which they actually relate.
- The figures for investment income have been similarly adjusted.
- While Example 25 shows the whole cost of buying equipment that will last ten years, Example 26 shows only one year's depreciation.

Example 25 Receipts and Payments Account for the year ended 31 August 1995

Year to 31.8.94 £	£		£	Year to 31.8.95 £
		Receipts		
	7,000	Fees	35,000	
	1,700	Other contributions	1,900	
	600	Investment income	3,400	
9,300				40,300
		Payments		
	1,500	Community services	1,600	
		Purchase of equipment	29,000	
	4,000	Residential care	5,000	
	1,800	Support services	1,900	
7,300				37,500
2,000		*Excess of receipts over payments*		2,800

Example 26 Income and Expenditure Account for the year ended 31 August 1995

Year to 31.8.94 £	£		£	Year to 31.8.95 £
		Income		
20,000		**1** Fees	22,000	
1,700		**2** Other contributions	1,900	
2,000		**3** Investment income	2,000	
23,700				25,900
		Expenditure		
1,500		**4** Community services	1,600	
		5 Depreciation of equipment	2,900	
4,000		**6** Residential care	5,000	
1,800		**7** Support services	2,000	
7,300				11,500
16,400		**8** *Excess of income over expenditure*		14,400

Note Items are numbered in this example to help you follow where they appear in Examples 28 and 29.

The Balance Sheet

Example 27 shows the Balance Sheet for the Receipts and Payments Account shown in Example 25, while the Balance Sheet for the Income and Expenditure Account shown in Example 26 is shown in Example 28. Where figures are shown in brackets, this means that they are negative.

The key difference is that with the Income and Expenditure Account we include debtors, creditors, stock and depreciation in the Balance Sheet. 'Debtors' in Example 28 refers to fees and investment income received in 1995 but which relate to 1994 (see Example 29).

Example 27 Balance Sheet accompanying Receipts and Payments Account

Balance Sheet as at 31 August 1995

31.8.94 £		31.8.95 £
	Assets	
26,500	Money at bank and in hand at beginning of year	28,500
2,000	Increase in money at bank and in hand during year	2,800
28,500	Money at bank and in hand at end of year	31,300
	Liabilities	
	Accumulated Fund: XYZ Fund	
26,500	Opening balance	28,500
2,000	Excess of receipts over payments	2,800
28,500	Closing balance	31,300

Example 28 Balance Sheet accompanying Income and Expenditure Account

Balance Sheet as at 31 August 1995

31.8.94 £			31.8.95 £
	Assets		
600	Stock		500
14,400	Debtors		
28,500	Money at bank and in hand		31,300
	Equipment	29,000	
	less depreciation	(2,900)	26,100
43,500			57,900
	Liabilities		
	Accumulated Fund: XYZ Fund		
26,100	Opening balance		43,500
16,400	**8** Excess of income over expenditure		14,400
43,500	Closing balance		57,900

Assets, in Example 28, have increased by £14,400 over the year. Does this relate to any other figure? Yes, the excess of income over expenditure shown under 'Liabilities'. So the increase in the assets equals the increase shown in the Income and Expenditure Account (Example 26).

Example 29 summarises how the adjustments which we make in the Income and Expenditure Account involve an apparent increase in 'income' (excess of receipts/income over payments/expenditure) of £11,600.

You will see that column **A** is your Receipts and Payments Account for the year ended 31 August 1995 (Example 25). The middle column shows the adjustments that are made to provide you with your Income and Expenditure Account **B** for the same year (Example 26).

The main reason for the increase in income of £11,600 is clearly that the purchase of equipment (£29,000) is not included in the Income and Expenditure Account because the equipment is not 'written off' in the year of purchase but instead capitalised (ie treated as an asset) and written off over the expected life of the asset as depreciation (ie it is 'depreciated' annually).

The income from support services increased from £1,900 in the Receipts and Payments Account to £2,000 in the Income and Expenditure Account. This is due to the fact that £100 of stock (eg clothes and blankets) was recorded at the year end; when added to the cash receipts of £1,900, this made a total of £2,000.

Example 29 How the Receipts and Payments Account is adjusted to produce the Income and Expenditure Account

	A		B
	Receipts and Payments Account	Adjustments (debtors, creditors, stock and depreciation)	Income and Expenditure Account
	£	£	£
1 Fees (debtor)	35,000	(13,000)	22,000
2 Other contributions	1,900	–	1,900
3 Investment income (debtor)	3,400	(1,400)	2,000
Total receipts/income	40,300	(14,400)	25,900
		(debtors)	
4 Community services	1,600	–	1,600
5 Purchase of equipment	29,000	(29,000)	–
5 Depreciation of equipment	–	2,900	2,900
6 Residential care	5,000	–	5,000
7 Support services (stock)	1,900	100	2,000
Total payments/expenditure	37,500	(26,000)	11,500
Excess of receipts/income over payments/expenditure	2,800	11,600	14,400

CHAPTER NINE

Keeping track of covenants

Deeds of covenant are used a great deal by charities because they can claim a tax rebate from the Inland Revenue on gifts made under covenant.

How covenants work
·········

Covenants are deeds made for four years or longer. Tax is reclaimed at the basic rate from donations received under deed of covenant. If this is 24 per cent, the charity reclaims £3.16 for every £10 received.

To calculate the **tax recoverable** on a given net annual amount (donation, subscription, etc) at any basic tax rate the following formula can be used:

$$\frac{\text{net annual amount receivable}}{(100 \text{ minus the basic tax rate})} \times \frac{\text{basic tax rate}}{1} = \text{tax recoverable}$$

If the net annual amount receivable is £10 and the basic rate of tax is 24 per cent, it works out at:

$$\frac{10}{(100-24)} \times \frac{24}{1} = £3.16$$

So the charity receives £10 (net amount) from the donor and £3.16 from the Inland Revenue, a total (gross) annual amount of £13.16.

The charity has a responsibility to ensure that the net amount received (£10 in the above example) *is* received. The Inland

Revenue may inspect the charity's books to see that the system is being operated correctly.

Some covenants (eg interest-free loans) are made where there is a 'one-off' gift to the charity under a four-year covenant. In this case the tax rebate is claimed as if the payment had been made in four equal annual instalments. For example, the receipt under the deed of covenant could be for £100. That is treated as £25 per annum and tax refunds of £7.89 per annum are claimed each year.

It is wise to keep a careful record of these tax refund claims: if you have a large number of them, it can become very confusing over a period of years.

Checking that the correct amounts are received

Treasurers should therefore **reconcile** the amount actually received from donors with the amount required under their deeds of covenant. The Inland Revenue allows small carry-over differences at the year end, but if the difference is large then the charity should ascertain the reason and follow up the matter with the donor before claiming the tax from the Inland Revenue. Example 30 compares the actual amounts received with the covenanted amounts.

Example 30 Comparison of actual amounts received with covenanted amounts

Covenant number	Receipts			Annual covenant total	(Under) or over-received
	1.4.93 to 31.8.93 £	1.9.93 to 31.3.94 £	Net total received £	£	£
3	40.00	60.00	100.00	100.00	–
5	10.00	15.00	25.00	25.00	–
7	5.00	7.50	12.50	13.00	(0.50)
9	25.00	35.00	60.00	60.00	–
12	7.50	10.50	18.00	20.00	(2.00)

Covenant number	Receipts			Annual covenant total	(Under) or over-received
	1.4.93 to 31.8.93 £	1.9.93 to 31.3.94 £	Net total received £	£	£
13	100.00	150.00	250.00	240.00	10.00
15	50.00	73.00	123.00	120.00	3.00
17	25.00	39.00	64.00	60.00	4.00
19	30.00	45.00	75.00	75.00	–
21	30.00	45.00	75.00	75.00	–
22	20.00	28.00	48.00	48.00	–
23	5.00	7.50	12.50	13.00	(0.50)
25	25.00	27.00	52.00	52.00	–
27	15.00	37.00	52.00	52.00	–
29	5.00	7.00	12.00	12.00	–
33	28.00	47.00	75.00	75.00	–
35	40.00	60.00	100.00	120.00	(20.00)
36	350.00	650.00	1,000.00	1,000.00	–
37	5.00	7.00	12.00	12.00	–
38	18.00	34.00	52.00	52.00	–
39	180.00	320.00	500.00	500.00	–
41	1,000.00	1,000.00	2,000.00	2,400.00	(400.00)
43	5.00	7.50	12.50	13.00	(0.50)
45	21.00	31.00	52.00	52.00	–
47	40.00	60.00	100.00	120.00	(20.00)
49	450.00	550.00	1,000.00	1,000.00	–
Total	2,529.50	3,353.00	5,882.50	6,309.00	(426.50)
	A	B	C	D	E
Cash book	2,529.50	4,678.45	7,207.95	7,207.95	–
	F	G	H	I	J
Difference	0.00	(1,325.45)	(1,325.45)	(898.45)	(426.50)
	K	L	M	N	O

The first three cash columns of Example 30 show the actual amount received, which may or may not have been recorded in the cash book. M is the difference (£1,325.45) between this 'actual amount received' (C = £5,882.50) and the amount shown in the cash book (H = £7,207.95). Example 31 shows how this difference is made up.

Example 31 How a discrepancy arises between amount recorded in cash book and amount actually received

Covenant number		£
52	cash received but deed not yet processed	250.00
54	cash received but deed not yet processed	56.00
55	cash received but deed not yet processed	12.50
59	cash received but deed not yet processed	89.00
60	cash received but deed not yet processed	438.00
	Total of cash received relating to deeds not yet processed	845.50
	Fees, in wrong column of cash book	479.95
		1,325.45

N in Example 30 is the difference of £898.95 between what should have been received and what the cash book showed; this is simply the difference between £1,325.45 (M) and the under-/over-receipts of £426.50 (O).

Column E shows a total of £426.50 net under-received. You will see that covenant numbers 7, 12, 23, 35, 43 and 47 show small under-payments, while covenant numbers 13, 15 and 17 show small over-payments. These can be left in the claim because the Inland Revenue allows small under- and over-receipts to be carried over from one tax year to the next.

Covenantor number 41 has left the area (or the country) and is no longer paying under the covenant. It is therefore wrong to claim a tax rebate on more than £2,000. The remaining £400 should be deducted from the claim.

Action plan

········

The action to be taken following this process of checking is as follows:

- Transfer £479.95 from the 'covenants' column of the cash book to the 'fees' column.
- Deal with the deeds not yet processed (£845.50) within the next claim.
- Reduce the current claim for covenant number 41 by £400 to £5,909.00.

The small remaining under-receipt of £26.50 will be noted but no action taken (ie it will be ignored as far as the claim is concerned).

Example 32 shows a reconciliation of covenants with cash received which incorporates all these adjustments.

Example 32 Reconciliation of covenants to cash received

	Cash book	Claim
Actual, as above	H 7,207.95	D 6,309.00
Deduct fees in wrong column of cash book	479.95	
Deduct covenants not yet processed	845.50	
	C 5,882.50	D 6,309.00
Reduce the claim by the amount which has not been received (number 41)		400.00
Net total received	C 5,882.50	5,909.00
Add small under-/over-receipts allowed in claim	26.50	
Balanced total	5,909.00	5,909.00

Glossary

Accounting convention A definition, or set of rules, accepted by accountants as applying to a given set of circumstances. For example, the 'historical cost convention' relates to valuing all items at their historical cost (a building cost £1 million to erect; it is, therefore, in the Balance Sheet at that cost, subject to depreciation).

Accrual *See under* Creditor.

Accumulated Fund An organisation has a responsibility to repay the exact value of its assets when it ceases to operate (winds up). On the liabilities side of the Balance Sheet there are amounts which exactly correspond to these assets. The assets will be sold and the amount distributed to those to whom it is due. If there are creditors (for goods and services already provided) or lenders of money, then these will be paid first. The remainder will be paid to whoever the trustees find are legally due to receive it. It is this remainder which is shown by the Accumulated Fund. It is the fund of assets which has accumulated so far.

Asset An item which has been acquired by or is due to the organisation (building, equipment, investments, money, debtors, stock). The value at which the asset is recorded in the Balance Sheet depends upon the 'accounting convention' employed.

Balance In 'double-entry bookkeeping', every debit has a corresponding credit. In a cash book or ledger account (eg a Bank Control Account), the difference between the left-hand side (the debit side) and the right-hand side (the credit side) is an amount needed to *balance* the two sides (the left-hand and right-hand sides must always equal each other). This balance is carried forward to the next financial period (as the cash-in-hand or other debt/asset or credit/liability). The *opening balance* in a ledger account is the balance at the beginning of the financial period. The *closing balance* is the balance at the end of the financial period.

Balance Sheet A statement or summary of all the closing balances (see 'Balance' above) as at the end of the financial period. As with each account in the ledger, the two sides of the Balance Sheet must equal each other. The balances included in the Balance Sheet are those of a capital nature; the balances relating to revenue items will have been brought together in the Receipts and Payments Account or the Income and Expenditure Account, the final balance on that account being shown in the Balance Sheet.

Bank Control Account A summary account in the charity's ledger which records, in summary form, all the transactions relating to a specific account at the bank. It is generally used only in the larger organisations, where several (or many hundreds of separate) lists, computer spreadsheets or columnar cash books are used to record bank receipts and payments. These are brought together to provide one unified 'balance', which can be reconciled with the bank statements from the bank.

Bank reconciliation It is very seldom that the last figure on the latest bank statement agrees with the 'closing balance' in your cash book or Bank Control Account. There will be items such as cheques which you have drawn but which have not been presented (paid by the bank) and deposits which you have put into the bank but which have not yet been credited. A bank reconciliation is a structured way in which to agree your records with those of the bank.

Bank statement A 'Statement of Account' issued by the bank which shows every transaction on your account as far as *their* records show. This statement may show charges, interest, direct debits or subscriptions received of which you are not aware. When the account has funds in it, available for your use, it is said to be 'in credit' (or 'in the black'). If it is overdrawn, you owe the bank the amount shown and it is said to be 'in debit/overdrawn' (or 'in the red').

Capital account *See under* Revenue account.

Cash In this handbook defined as notes and coins. 'Bank' items, such as cheques, credit cards, standing orders, direct debits and other methods of transacting business which pass primarily through the bank clearing system, are called 'money at bank'. The term 'cash in hand and at bank' (when used in a Balance Sheet) includes both 'cash' and 'money at bank'.

Cash book A columnar book in which receipts and/or payments are recorded. The term will include a computer spreadsheet or other database record.

Cash Control Account A summary account in the charity ledger which records, in summary form, all 'cash' transactions. It is generally used only where several separate lists, computer spreadsheets or columnar books are used to record cash receipts and payments; these are then brought together to provide one unified 'balance', which can be reconciled with the actual cash-in-hand.

Cash float or imprest A fixed amount, sufficient to cover cash payments made over a period of time (eg a month, three months). When the float is run down, a claim is made for the amount spent in order to increase the amount of cash held back to the full value of the float.

Cash flow forecast Figures which show how much money will be available at a given date or dates in the future (similar to a series of budget statements). (Not related to a Cash Flow Statement.)

Cash flow statement A financial statement, used by large organisations, to show how the 'increase in cash and cash equivalents' has changed the monetary position from the beginning to the end of the financial period (eg from 1 September 1994 to 31 August 1995). It reconciles the

Income and Expenditure Account to the money-only turnover for the year (which is your Receipts and Payments Account). Smaller organisations are better served by an Income and Expenditure Account (or Receipts and Payments Account) and Balance Sheet.

Cash-in-hand Cash (notes and coin) physically held at a given date.

Cash reconciliation A structured way in which to agree the actual cash-in-hand to the 'balance' shown in your cash book or Cash Control Account.

Covenant A legal document whereby the covenantor promises to make a payment or payments, usually over a four-year period. The charity can claim income tax from the Inland Revenue if the covenantor is a taxpayer.

Credit balance The credit balance on a bank statement is money in a bank account which the bank is liable to pay to the customer who has funds in that account. A charity's credit balance is the net amount shown in a ledger on the credit (right-hand) side. It is an amount which may be due to someone else. 'Revenue' balances, such as fees, donations received or income from sales will be on the credit side until the end of the financial period, when they will form part of the 'excess of receipts over payments' (or vice versa) in the Receipts and Payments Account, or the 'Excess of income over expenditure' (or vice versa) in the Income and Expenditure Account. 'Capital' balances (Accumulated Fund, loans, amounts due as creditors) will appear in the Balance Sheet as 'Liabilities'.

Creditor A person or organisation to whom money is due. It is a credit balance in a ledger which is carried forward at a particular date and will be shown in the Balance Sheet as a liability. Included in the term 'creditor' will be 'accruals' (amounts, like interest on a loan, which *accrue* regularly from day to day; although relating to the current financial period, they will not be paid until the next) and 'provisions' (amounts, such as charges for gas or electricity, which have not yet been paid but are *provided* for in the current year's

Income and Expenditure Account and Balance Sheet).
Accruals and provisions (sometimes the terms are used
synonymously) are included in the current period in order to
provide a 'true and fair view' of expenditure for the period.

Debit balance In a ledger account, the debit side is the left-hand
side. If the value of the items on the debit side exceeds those
on the credit side of the account, then there is a debit balance
on that account. Bank statements record figures in terms of
their ledger, so a debit balance on a bank statement implies
that you owe the bank money – hence an overdraft in terms
of your (the charity) bank account.

Debtor A person or organisation that owes money to the
charity. The term can be extended, when quoted in the
Balance Sheet, to include 'prepayments'. In this wider
context the word 'debtor' includes all 'debit balances'
carried forward in the ledger accounts at the end of a
financial period (the Balance Sheet date).

Deposit Money paid into a bank (deposited).

Depreciation The cost of buildings, furniture and fittings, and
equipment divided equally over its estimated life. Each year
the annual amount is charged as 'depreciation' in the
Income and Expenditure Account. In the year in which it is
sold or scrapped, an adjustment will be made to take account
of any money received when that occurs.

Double-entry bookkeeping A system of keeping records of
financial transactions (receipts and payments, accruals and
prepayments) where every item recorded on the debit side
has a corresponding item on the credit side.

Endowment funds or **Permanent endowment funds** Capital
funds held by a charity. The income from the capital can be
used but the trustees have no power to convert the capital
into income.

Gift Aid Tax relief for single monetary (cheque, bank transfer
or credit card) gifts made to UK charities by UK residents.
From 16 March 1993, each gift must be at least £250 after
basic-rate tax is taken off.

Imprest *See* Cash float.

Income and Expenditure Account A Receipts and Payments Account with the addition of stock, creditors and debtors outstanding at the beginning and end of the period, and depreciation. An Income and Expenditure Account is, in effect, the Profit and Loss Account of a non-trading organisation.

Investment income Interest or dividends earned from investments, including shares, government stock, and money in building society or bank accounts.

Ledger account In double-entry bookkeeping a ledger is a book (or computer record) in which there are a number of 'ledger accounts', each of which records specific items of financial value. All the ledger accounts, taken together, will record every aspect of the financial affairs of the organisation.

Liability An amount which the organisation will have to pay out in the future. The following are examples of liabilities: loans which were made to the organisation (including 'interest-free loans' under covenant), mortgages (where they are amounts owing to creditors), bank overdraft, sundry creditors (for goods and services purchased but not yet paid for), Accumulated Fund, share capital (eg of a limited liability company).

Money at bank The funds available at the bank as shown by your records (not the bank statement).

Net The result after taking one figure from another, eg gross salary, less income tax, leaves net salary.

Overdraft A facility granted by a bank whereby you owe money to the bank. The bank account will be in debit ('in the red').

Payments Cash and money which have actually been paid out in the financial period; *not* the same as 'expenditure'.

Prepayment Where a payment (or part of a payment) which relates to a later period has been made in one financial period, only that part which relates to the current period should be recorded in the Income and Expenditure Account; that part which relates to the next period should be carried forward as a 'prepayment'. It will be a debit balance, carried down in a ledger account, and must be recorded as an asset in the Balance Sheet.

Provision   *see under* Creditor.

Receipts   Cash and money which have actually been received in the financial period; *not* the same as 'income'.

Receipts and Payments Account   An account which summarises all receipts and all payments for a given financial period (usually a year). It should provide useful information about how much was received for specific items (eg fees, sales, donations, covenants, etc) and how much was paid out for specific items. It may show an 'excess of receipts over payments' or an 'excess of payments over receipts' for the accounting period.

Reimbursement   An amount repaid or due to be repaid. The term generally relates to the amount needed to bring a cash float back to the amount originally granted.

Restricted funds   Funds that are received by a charity for a specific purpose, stated by the donor, and must be spent only for that purpose.

Revenue account   There are two kinds of account, revenue and capital. Revenue accounts are debited or credited to the Receipts and Payments Account or the Income and Expenditure Account in the financial period to which they relate. Capital accounts are of a more permanent nature and represent amounts carried forward in the Balance Sheet to the next financial period.

Stock   Tangible items which remain in the possession of the organisation at the end of the financial period. This includes items for resale; advertising leaflets, stationery and other objects used for administrative purposes; food. It should be included in the accounts at a 'true and fair' value (various 'accounting conventions' dictate different methods of valuation).

Tax year From 6 April in one year to 5 April in the next. It is the financial period employed by the Inland Revenue in which income is deemed to arise.

Unrestricted funds Funds that are expendable at the discretion of the trustees in furtherance of the objects of the charity.

Withdrawal In the context of bank transactions, it is the opposite of a 'deposit': you take money out of the bank (withdraw it).

Charity Commission publications
·········

The Charity Commission has a wide range of publications on the duties of charity trustees and the accounting requirements of charities. All except ACC-1371 (on the SORP) are available free of charge from any of its three offices (addresses opposite). Publications include:

CC3 *Responsibilities of Charity Trustees.*

CC32 *Trustee Investments Act 1961 – A guide.*

CC51 *Charity Accounts: The new framework* (November 1995).

CC52 *Charity Accounts: Charities under the £10,000 threshold,* available from 1 April 1996. This sets out the accounting requirements for charities with neither income nor expenditure over £10,000.

CC53 *Charity Accounts: Charities over the £10,000 threshold,* available from 1 April 1996. This sets out the accounting requirements for all charities with either income or expenditure over £10,000.

Standard Accounts Forms will be included in CC52 and CC53; they are also available separately.

CC1 lists all Charity Commission publications.

ACC-1371 *Accounting by Charities: Statement of Recommended Practice (SORP).* This should be sent to all registered charities free of charge. Additional copies £5.

Charity Commission offices

St Alban's House
57–60 Haymarket
London SW1Y 4QX
Tel 0171-210 4556

2nd Floor
20 Kings Parade
Queens Dock
Liverpool L3 4DQ
Tel 0151-703 1500

Woodfield House
Tangier
Taunton
Somerset TA1 4BL
Tel 01823 345000

Index